The Trumpet of *His Coming*

Joseph Karasanyi

ISBN 978-1-64670-527-6 (Paperback)
ISBN 978-1-64670-528-3 (Digital)

Covenant Books, Inc.
11661 Hwy 707
Murrells Inlet, SC 29576
www.covenantbooks.com

Contents

Foreword

"In the twenty-first century Christians find the tenacity of their faith tested as they are pulled in multiple directions. The road of sanctification is littered with many who start highly committed to Christ but, like seed planted in shallow soil, wither when other interests and concerns overtake hearts and minds.

The Church's message to the world is Good News, the Gospel of Jesus Christ, the risen Lord. We are not called to please men, but to build the Kingdom of God, all in Jesus' name.

There are any number of modern eschatological texts for sale online. Most, however, are scholarly treaties for the academy. It is enjoyable when you find a book for the average layperson in the pew or for the God seeking pre-Christian. *The Trumpet of His Coming* is just that type of text.

Bishop Joseph Karasanyi's unorthodox, but interesting presentation of three comings of Christ notwithstanding, the text is Scripture rich and readable. His gift of exhortation shines through with probing questions demanding the reader examine ministries and motives. A prayerful reading of this book would be spiritually profitable for pastors and laypeople alike."

Dr. Dale C. Williams
Boone, North Carolina

Introduction

When a trumpet is blown, its sound indicates a variety of messages. Trumpet-like instruments have historically been used to call worshippers to assemble, warriors to battle, or hunters to the hunting grounds; but in the Word of God, a trumpet was used to warn the people of impending danger or to alert them that something unusual was about to happen.

> He heard the sound of the trumpet and did not take warning; His blood shall be upon himself. But if he had taken warning, he would have saved his life. (Ezekiel 33:5)

In our day, as a people waiting for the coming of our Lord Jesus, the sound of a trumpet will be used by angels on God's command to gather His elect people from the corners of the earth for the final assembly; as it is written in the book of Matthew,

> And he will send out his angels with a loud trumpet call, and they will gather his elect from the four winds, from one end of heaven to the other.

In this book, the trumpet of His coming is not in the form of loud sounds. It is the trumpet of the written Word still serving the same purpose of warning, awakening, and alerting mankind about Jesus's coming. The urgency in the sound of the trumpet signals that this will be very soon. This trumpet of His coming conveys a strong message written in the simplest way, very easy, and very clear to be understood by everyone who will have an opportunity to read the message in this book.

And this trumpet of His coming is for the whole body of Christ who are eagerly waiting with renewed hope for the triumphant return of our Lord Jesus Christ.

This book, *The Trumpet of His Coming*, is to help you prepare yourself and your ministry before we hear the final blowing of the angel's thunderous trumpet. As it is written in the book of Matthew,

> And he will send his angels with a great sound of
> a trumpet, and they will gather together His elect
> from the four winds from one end of heaven to
> the other. (Matthew 24:31)

1

The Trumpet of His Coming

In the context of this book, *The Trumpet of His Coming* is focused on the last coming of Jesus Christ. Nonetheless, it starts with two other different occasions of His coming.

You may ask yourself, how many times has Jesus had to come back physically? The Bible tells us about the coming of Christ. And there are more than two different comings on two different occasions which are evident in the whole mission of our Lord Jesus Christ.

Before we talk about different occasions of His coming, we have to remember the truth about the mission of our Lord Jesus. The truth is that from the beginning of time, our Lord Jesus was there. That was before His first coming physically to this world. He was the Word of God and was with God.

> In the beginning was, the Word, and the Word was with God, and the Word was God. The same was at the beginning with God. All things were made by him; and without him was not anything made that was made. (John 1:1–4)

This is the truth of the Word of God about Jesus Christ, what He was, what He is, and will be; He is greater than the times and seasons. When Jesus came to the world, He came with a special mission. This mission was given to Him by His heavenly Father.

Our Lord Jesus's whole mission was divided into three parts, and each part had main activities to be accomplished as we are going to see in this book.

His mission had three different phases. Each phase served a special purpose (set of activities) to be accomplished, as we are going to see from the Word of God.

His was indeed a special mission with a specific work plan and a specified time frame.

> But I have greater witness than that of John: For the works which the Father hath given me to finish, the same works that I do, bear witness of me, that the Father has sent me. (John 5:36)

This scripture is confirming the special mission of our Lord Jesus that was given him by his heavenly Father in heaven as we are going to see in this book.

Our heavenly Father loved the world with a great heavenly love. He loved mankind even though the man was so sinful. Our heavenly Father planned this mission when He decided to send His only Son to save mankind. This mission had a lot of challenges and hard times, but thus how God planned it. It was a test of a lifetime. It was a demonstration of love beyond understanding—giving away a sinless Son to pay ransom for a world full of remorseless serial sinners!

2

The First Coming of Our Lord Jesus

Many people have talked and written about the first and second coming of Jesus Christ. In this book, however, we are going to talk also about Christ's first, second and third coming. We have witnessed Christ's first and second coming; therefore, we are waiting for the third coming of Jesus. As we read through the pages of this book, we are bound to discover which of these comings we are actually waiting for. The first, second and third coming of Jesus are found in the Word of God—the Bible. The main issue is not how many times Jesus is coming back; what is most important in this message is the fact that Jesus is coming back very soon—sooner than you can imagine.

As we read, we are going to see and find out which is the first coming, the second, and the last coming. And all these different comings are mentioned in the Word of God as written in the Bible. The first coming of Christ into the world was prophesied by the Prophet Isaiah:

> Therefore the Lord himself shall give you a sign;
> Behold, a virgin shall conceive, and bear a son,
> and shall call his name Emmanuel. (Isaiah 7:14)

And again the prophet says,

> For unto us a child is born, unto us a son is given: and the government shall be upon his shoulder: and his name shall be called Wonderful Counselor, the mighty God, the everlasting Father and, the Prince of Peace. (Isaiah 9:6)

These prophetic words were repeatedly cited in different chapters and verses in the Book of Isaiah. This was the trumpet of the first coming of Jesus. It was sounded through Isaiah's prophecies many years before Jesus. Regardless of time lag, Jesus finally came. We will talk about the timing of each coming later as we go deep in our book. This first coming took place when Jesus Christ was born in Bethlehem and came into this world physically like any other human being.

> For unto you is born this day in the city of David
> a Savior, which is Christ the Lord. (Luke 2: 11)

This was witnessed by the shepherds, wise men, and the angels. These angels had a special massage to the shepherds (Luke 2:10–12).

With all sound of the trumpets through the prophecies of different prophets, it was made clear that the son is on the way coming. But the people of that time were like people of this time; some believed in coming of the Son, the Messiah, and some didn't believe. But everybody was aware of the coming of the Messiah from the trumpet of prophecies. This book is a trumpet in your hand with the sound of his coming.

Part 1 of First Coming: Jesus's Ministries

The main activities in the mission of Jesus Christ's first coming were threefold: The first was to introduce the world to the heavenly kingdom of His Father. The second was to teach and train His *disciples*, transforming them from fishermen to teachers and writers, from tax collectors to apostles, and preparing them for the coming big task of worldwide mission. The third was to willingly die on the cross at Calvary so as to save mankind from the bondage and slavery and spiritual death inherited from Adam when he sinned in the garden of Eden. The above major ministries had to be done in a specific period of time.

In this first coming of his coming, the ministry went on for three years and ended the first part of His mission, which was concluded upon the cross at Calvary, where He paid the ransom saving mankind from the devil's bondage. We have to note that each coming was accompanied by a special and specific ministry or task that had to be accomplished according to God's plan.

We see that the purpose of Jesus's first assignment was accomplished in the first coming, and indeed, this was part one of the great mission. There were three main activities as mentioned earlier, namely:

- Doing evangelism of going out and reaching out for souls to introduce the heavenly kingdom—the Trinity of Father, Son, and Holy Spirit.
- To teach, recruit, and train disciples with a cardinal aim of transforming the lost human beings to children of God and make them ready to be used by God in His perfect plan.
- To die on the cross and redeem all mankind, destroy and render null and void the works of the devil and, at the same time, pay the price of His blood to take away the sins of mankind once and for all.

His shameful death on the cross marked the end of part one but certainly the great mission was still in progress. It was the beginning of sorting out things. As it is written in the Word of God that:

> He that committed sin is of the devil; for the devil sinned from the beginning. For this purpose, the Son of God was manifested that he might destroy the works of the devil. (1 John 3:8)

Our Lord Jesus did all the work of part one of the mission according to the blueprint made in heaven by the Father in His master plan. This episode came to a close on the cross when Jesus himself blew the whistle to signal an end to the first phase. "It is finished," he said.

> When Jesus therefore had received the vinegar, he said, It is finished: And he bowed his head, and gave up the Spirit. (John 19:30)

By this time according to the scripture, when Jesus said it's finished, it means his first assignment of the part of the mission was finished.

This was His heavenly Father's plan and His will. Jesus confirmed this in the garden shortly before going to the cross when He said:

> "Abba, Father," he said, "everything is possible for you. Take this cup from me. Yet not what I will, but what you will." (Mark 14:36)

This part of paying the price was very hard and extremely painful to the heavenly Father who watched His only begotten Son go through this very undeserving painful torture. This serves as a fulfillment of the gospel as written by John, the great evangelist.

> For God so loved the world that he gave His only begotten son, that whoever believes in Him should not perish but have everlasting life. (John 3:16)

And it was too painful to Jesus himself as it stated in scripture when He wished that if possible, the cup be taken away. But after going through severe pain which culminated unto His death, this part of the mission came to an end. The first part of the first coming came to a logical conclusion, and it was a done deal.

As we all know from Jesus's words, His mission came from His heavenly Father's plan. And the heavenly Father was in full control of the Son's mission. The Son's mission is written in the book of John 5:36 when he said, "I have greater witness than John's; for the works which the Father has given me to finish—the very work I do—bear witness of me, that the Father has send me."

That marked the end of the first coming and the first part of the great mission. Jesus did all that was supposed to be done during that first part of the mission. At that time, all left Him to suffer an ignoble death on the cruel cross. During this torturous time and eventual demise of the Master, everybody had lost hope, but ironically His death on the cross was set to permanently transform history: the present and future of mankind.

3

The Most Painful Moment to the Father and the Son

In most cases, people teach and write about the pain and agony Jesus went through on the way to Calvary and pain on the cross. But in this book, we are going to see the painful moment both to our God, heavenly Father, and the Son Jesus Christ went through in the same boat of pain.

Both our Lord Jesus and His Father went through a serious and painful moment. The simple evidence that Jesus was in deep pain was when He asked His Father to take away the cup (*agony*).

> Going a little farther, he fell with his face to the ground and prayed, "My Father, if it is possible, may this cup be taken from me. Yet not as I will, but as you will." (Matthew 26:39)

At that moment, His Father heard His prayer, and He understood what His Son was going through. But the mighty Father didn't say any word because the decision had been taken in heaven: "God so loved the world that He gave His only Son as ransom for the sin of mankind."

After checking on His disciples for the second time, Jesus focused on His Father's will, confirming the fact that God so loved

JOSEPH KARASANYI

the world. He went away a second time and prayed that God's will be done. But it is not possible for this cup to be taken away. Jesus had to drink it; God's will had to be done on earth as it was in heaven.

> He went away a second time and prayed, "My Father, if it is not possible for this cup to be taken away unless I drink it, may your will be done." (Matthew 26:42)

Jesus was very clear and open about how He felt, when He said to them,

> My soul is overwhelmed with sorrow to the point of death, stay here and keep watch with me. (Matthew 26:38)

The situation became even worse and more painful as death loomed largely. Jesus cried to the Father, who from all human angles seemed to have forsaken Him. This was a serious, desperate communication between Father and Son. It was too painful to the Son and certainly to the heavenly Father too.

There is only one logical reason for this behavior where a mighty Father allows an innocent Son to die like a common robber: Because God so loved the world that He gave His only Son.

You simply have to stretch your imagination to internalize how much the almighty God loved His Son and above that is His love for mankind. Mankind needs to ponder on how much power He can command. He who created heaven and earth and holds the power of life and death in His hands had to stand and watch His Son killed. This is the mother of all mysteries! Yes, you need to have a son; you also need to have power at your disposal to save Him and yet watch sinners hack him to death for a crime He has not committed. Indeed, there must have been a lot of darkness to blind the world to the cruel realities of that day. You need all this to understand this moment! Indeed, you need to be a mother or a father to understand the predicament.

No wonder even the sky that day felt the shock. From noon until three in the afternoon, darkness came over all the land. Jesus cried out in a loud voice. I would like you to understand Jesus at this time; it wasn't just prayer, but a loud cry full of pain and agony.

> "Eli, Eli, [some manuscripts "Eloi, Eloi] lema sabachthani?" Which means "My God, my God, why have you forsaken me?" (Matthew 27:46)

The only Son pleading to a Father that seems to have forsaken Him, and the Father turns his face away to a cruel death on the cross of shame is a situation not common to man. That the Father heard this cry but felt powerless to act is the single indicator that He loved His son but loved the human race more! This shows the moment of reckoning for the Father and Son. It is the furnace *God the Father and God the Son* went through to redeem you and me from the death and eternal slavery the devil had sentenced us to. Indeed, God so loved the world the way only He can afford!

If one didn't at all know the cost of his salvation, this is it. This is how unconditionally God loved you and me! The love is too powerful to be understood using human calculations. That is how heavenly God's love is for those that believe in Him.

Such is the solemnity of His love. Indeed, love beyond understanding. It is this same love which is bringing Him back. To reward and to take to heaven those that loved and obeyed Him is central to this critical mission.

When our Lord Jesus with a crown of thorns around His head bled on the cross at Calvary, it wasn't fun. It was not business as usual. This was a great price He had to pay for the salvation of man. That is why none should take salvation for granted. At that particular

19

moment, you were on his heart, when he was overbleeding on the cross from his head to his feet. Whatever he went through and whatever he did it for you and me. Just for you, think about that value which was given to you by the grace.

At this time, the prophet Isaiah's prophecy was fulfilled.

> He was despised and rejected by mankind, a man of suffering, and familiar with suffering like one from whom men hide their faces, he was despised and we esteemed him not. Surely he took up our pain and bore our suffering, yet we considered him punished by God, stricken by him, and afflicted. But he was pierced for our transgressions, he was crushed for our iniquities; the punishment that brought us peace was on him, and by his wounds we are healed. (Isaiah 53:3–5)

This pain and agony Jesus went through is the main reason behind the Holy Communion. Jesus mentions two pillars of faith: His body and His blood. He knew many people would forget and even ignore what He went through and the price He paid for our salvation.

Jesus was very clear and open about how He felt on the cross when He said that His soul was overwhelmed. The truth is, there is no way you can measure the value of our salvation, and above all, we were given this salvation for free by grace.

As Apostle Paul witnessed about himself, giving an example of who he was and how by the grace of God received the salvation, which he said that he did not deserve it because of his renowned behavior of persecuting the church. Like everybody among us, we can remember and know where God brought us from to his salvation and become a child of God. Try to understand the value of our salvation.

For I am the least of the apostles and do not even deserve to be called an apostle, because I persecuted the church of God. But by the grace of God I am what I am, and his grace to me was not without effect. No, I worked harder than all of them—yet not I, but the grace of God that was with me. (1Cor15:9–10)

Toady when you are buying some items or looking for some service in a bank, they will ask to find out background check about you. If Jesus was to look for our background checks I believe none of us was to crucify to be loved. thank God, when God loved us, he didn't ask us for background checks, he didn't ask me where I come from, he didn't ask me my color not even my education. Didn't ask me for papers. He just loved me as Paul witness, we didn't deserve it but by the grace of God He loved us.

4

Jesus's Coming Back to Life Was His Second Coming

As the scriptures had loudly proclaimed, Jesus's coming back for the second part of His mission was His resurrection from the grave. This coming was indeed different from the first coming.

Jesus Christ prophesied to His disciples when He said He will go and would come back on the third day. His disciples could not understand where He was going, and the whole group of disciples asked their master where He was actually going.

> "Where are you going, Lord?" Simon Peter asked him. "You cannot follow me now where I am going," answered Jesus; "But later you will follow me." (John 13:36)

Jesus Christ was talking about His going and coming back to His disciples; that is the reason why Peter kept asking Jesus where He was going. Jesus didn't mention much or put emphasis on dying because His death was just a passage to where He was going. Death was therefore a means but not an end in itself. Jesus's conversation with His disciples about His going and His coming back naturally created confusion and brought about heated arguments among the disciples who looked at all this from a human perspective.

It is true they were very much worried about their master leaving them. It was their first time to be left alone without their master. The truth was, Jesus had to leave them and had to come back as He promised.

So when Jesus was arrested and killed on the cross at Calvary Hill, His disciples were engulfed by an intense fear that was worse than the fear they had had when a storm threatened their lives on lake Galilee.

He who had calmed the tempest was now dead and buried in a tomb lent to Him by Joseph of Arimathea. His tomb was heavily guarded by merciless Roman soldiers serving a government that wanted Him dead and forgotten. Things were as bad as that. Hopelessness loomed largely!

Simon Peter, the chief disciple, had denied Him three times just before the cock crowed, and Judas Iscariot who kept the purse had betrayed Him and later succumbed to an ignoble death of suicide. The young man John Mark that had followed Jesus had run away naked having dropped his cloak behind for fear of identification.

The meeting in the garden of Gethsemane had ended in disarray, and the whole ministry looked, for all intents and purposes, to have come to an immediate bitter end. They had seen with their very own eyes the end of an era: the death of the Messiah who was supposed to be the Redeemer of the wicked human race. They had witnessed a calamity in the true sense of the word! They started asking themselves with immense disappointments why this had come to pass. Even with the assurance they had been given by Jesus, they still wondered how this tragedy could happen, and how could one dead and buried possibly come to life again?

This was an issue of fundamental importance. It was too deep to fathom. Certainly not by a group of disciples most of whom had been mere fishermen that followed their master by simple faith in His word. They knew they were now on their own, and their only resort was to fight hard to avoid immediate arrest, death, and destruction. The odds against them were too many. They sat between the hammer and the anvil! Between life and death!

They therefore quickly scampered into the nearest nooks to hide from shame and imminent arrest. To them, this was doomsday! No wonder darkness had come at noon, and the curtain at the temple altar had torn apart! His disciples had been left with nothing, no power and no authority and not even simple guidelines for ministry. Theirs was a ship without a compass, a voyage without maps toward a destination that was unknown. They waited for the mother of all miracles to happen, but this too was hoping against hope. Three days became a century of despondency!

Jesus had left them without any plan. They had no sense of direction; they were full of terror of what was going to happen to their lives. They had nowhere to go. They were like vulnerable orphans abandoned on the roadside or defenseless sheep without a shepherd.

Away from a group of helpless disciples, Jesus left this world using death as a passage as He had many times told the disciples that had been unable to take Him by His word. This too was part of His mission whose aim was to defeat the devil and his demonic strategies. Jesus was gone for three days as it was planned and written by the infallible Word of God. He came back on the third day. His resurrection is common knowledge to all.

As we see, some discussion took place between the angel and the women who came to see the place where they thought they would find His body.

> But the angel said to the women, "Do not be afraid, for I know that you seek Jesus who was crucified. He is not here, for he has risen, as he said. Come, see the place where he lay. Then go quickly and tell

his disciples that he has risen from the dead, and
behold, he is going before you to Galilee; there you
will see him. See, I have told you." (Mark 16:6–7)

In very simple language, resurrection means to come back to
life after death. Jesus died on the cross for the sins of all mankind, but
He came back to life three days later. This was the second coming of
Jesus Christ on this earth. He went miserably but returned in total
victory and power as the guards witnessed.

And behold, there was a great earthquake, for an
angel of the Lord descended from heaven and came
and rolled back the stone and sat on it. His appear-
ance was like lightning, and his clothing white as
snow. And for fear of him the guards trembled and
became like dead men. (Matthew 28:2–4)

But let us first look at the difference between the normal defini-
tions of the word *resurrection*. Resurrection's meaning is when somebody dies and comes back to life with the body he had before his
death. That same body regains life and starts to function again, back
to life.

With Jesus, the difference was noticeable. When our Lord Jesus
came back to life, His body had been supernaturally transformed. He
was not like Lazarus and others who came back tied in burial clothes.
His was a super body that displayed the glory of a second coming. It
wasn't like any other resurrection!

When the centurion and those who were with
him, keeping watch over Jesus, saw the earthquake and what took place, they were filled
with awe and said, "Truly this was the Son of
God!" There were also many women there, looking on from a distance, who had followed Jesus
from Galilee, ministering to him, among whom

JOSEPH KARASANYI

were Mary Magdalene and Mary the mother of James and Joseph and the mother of the sons of Zebedee. (Matthew 27:54–55)

The above point is brought out more clearly in the gospel of Luke. Our Lord Jesus went to paradise where He met the criminal who was on cross with Him that day before His body was taken by Joseph of Arimathea to be buried.

> Then he said, "Jesus, remember me when you come into your kingdom." Jesus answered him, "Truly I tell you, and today you will be with me in paradise." (Luke 23:42–43)

That meant that on the same day Jesus went to paradise. Notably, he didn't mention His next destination after meeting the criminal man. He was still going on according to the plans of His heavenly Father.

Again we remember that when Jesus came back to this world on this occasion, He had not yet returned to His Father in heaven, He came back to this world before going to His father as revealed in John's gospel: what Jesus told Mary.

> Jesus said, "Do not hold on to me, for I have not yet ascended to the Father. Go instead to my brothers and tell them, 'I am ascending to my Father and your Father, to my God and your God.'" (John 20:17)

The above is also justified by the report of the guards who were guarding the tomb. These guards were eyewitnesses of Jesus's power over death. They witnessed the resurrection in broad daylight.

> The guards were so afraid of him that they shook and became like dead men. (Matthew 28:4)

26

The guards were afraid because of what they saw. These guards went to the city to report to the chief priest what they saw.

> While the women were on their way, some of the guards went into the city and reported to the chief priests everything that had happened. When the chief priests had met with the elders and devised a plan, they gave the soldiers a large sum of money, telling them, "You are to say, 'His disciples came during the night and stole him away while we were asleep.' If this report gets to the governor, we will satisfy him and keep you out of trouble." So the soldiers took the money and did as they were instructed. And this story has been widely circulated among the Jews to this very day. (Matthew 28:11–15)

Jesus appears to the disciples. John confirms it when he says:

> On the evening of that first day of the week, when the disciples were together, with the doors locked for fear of the Jewish leaders, Jesus came and stood among them and said, "Peace be with you!" After he said this, he showed them his hands and side. The disciples were overjoyed when they saw the Lord. (John 20:19–20)

This same situation is strengthened elsewhere in the gospels.

> While they were still talking about this, Jesus himself stood among them and said to them, "Peace be with you." They were startled and frightened, thinking they saw a ghost. He said to them, "Why are you troubled, and why do doubts rise in your minds? Look at my hands and my feet. It is I myself! Touch me and see; a

ghost does not have flesh and bones, as you see I have. When he had said this, he showed them his hands and feet. (Luke 24:36–40, NIV)

They thought they were seeing a ghost. But Jesus was clearly identifying Himself to His disciples and to the world at large that He was indeed physically alive.

By appearing to many different people in different places, our Lord Jesus confirmed His victory to make them believe and acknowledge His resurrection.

Jesus Christ our Lord did all it takes to show Himself to the world after coming back because He knew if He didn't show up, it would be too hard and difficult for people including His disciples to believe in His coming back (resurrection). That is why Jesus said to Thomas,

Because you have seen me, you have believed; blessed are those who have not seen and yet have believed. (John 20:29, NIV)

Thomas and his friends believed in the resurrection after seeing Jesus standing in their midst. When He came back, the Bible tells us He appeared to many people, but they could not recognize Him. In His new body, Jesus could go through the walls and roofs and could appear to different places possibly at the same time. Even His enemies could not arrest Him in that body.

This is again revealed by what happened when two men were walking while talking to each other on the road to Emmaus.

They were talking with each other about everything that had happened. As they talked and discussed these things with each other, Jesus himself came up and walked along with them, but they were kept from recognizing him. (Luke 24:14–16)

This new body was more powerful with glory than the first body before the crucifixion.

Jesus came back on this second coming the second time. This coming was vital and very important. You can imagine if Jesus had stayed dead and remained in the grave, we would still be under the punishment and power of sin, which is death.

> For the wages of sin is death, but the gift of God is eternal life in or through Christ Jesus our Lord. (Romans 6:23)

But Jesus Christ proved His victory over sin and death by coming back to life.

> I will deliver these people from the power of the grave; I will redeem them from death. Where, O death, are your plagues? Where, O grave, is your destruction? (Hosea 13:14, NIV)

The prophecy being fulfilled:

> Where, O death, is your victory? Where, O death, is your sting? The sting of death is sin, and the power of sin is the law. But thanks be to God! He gives us the victory through our Lord Jesus Christ. (1 Corinthians 15:55–57, NIV)

We have three points we have to put together which help us to believe that our Lord Jesus left this world and went on a journey which He himself was not in position to explain or reveal in detail to His disciples

When Jesus was talking to His disciples about His going, giving them a farewell, He was preparing them to stand by themselves without Him. The disciples were used to going with Jesus, and in the same way, they wanted to go with Him. So they kept on asking where He was going because He was seriously going away.

> My children, I will be with you only a little longer. You will look for me, and just as I told the Jews, so I tell you now: Where I am going, you cannot come. (John 13:33, NIV)

This scripture is very clear. It means he left and went, and the distance doesn't matter or how long he took to come back, but he left.

Jesus made a clear and loud appointment to one of the criminals who were on a cross beside him. Jesus said to him, "Tonight, we will be together in paradise." That tells us that on that same night, when He died on the cross, His journey was in progress. Nobody knows where He went after meeting the criminal man in paradise. As we see in the Word of God in the gospel of Luke:

> We are punished justly, for we are getting what our deeds deserve. But this man has done nothing wrong. Then he said, "Jesus, remember me when you come into your kingdom." Jesus answered him, "Truly I tell you, today you will be with me in paradise." (Luke 23:41–43, NIV)

Jesus's answer when He was asked where was he going? You can't go with Me now, but later when I come back, you will see Me.

Simon Peter asked him, "Lord, where are you going?" Jesus replied, "Where I am going, you cannot follow now, but you will follow later." Peter was still insisting to go. Because at that time, Peter had no idea of that journey. Peter asked, "Lord, why can't I follow you now? I will lay down my life for you." (John 13:36–37, NIV)

With these three points, we can agree that our Lord Jesus went away from this world and left a promise of coming back to His disciples.

Note this point: This was the first farewell, Jesus talking to His disciples when He was going away; exactly where, He didn't explain in detail. But after coming back, in the second farewell, as you are going to find out in this book, Jesus was so detailed about where He was going, starting with, "I'm going to the Father." Jesus was going away for the second time. His farewell was specifically going to his Father, and this was the second time going away from his disciples. This farewell, where Jesus mentioned that he's going to the Father, was the secondary farewell going back to his father.

His coming back to life from the grave marks the second coming of Christ Jesus and was done two thousand years ago. Nevertheless, the Bible continuously confirms and testifies very clearly that Jesus will come again. This should not confuse you. The whole mission of our Lord Jesus has three times of coming and three times of going back:

> First, Jesus came by the birth
> Second, he left this world through his death
> Third, he came back to this world through res-
> urrection
> Fourth, he left back to heaven to his heavenly
> Father
> Fifth, he is coming back very soon for the third
> time with reward and take us
> Sixth, he will go back, taking us where he has
> prepared places for us

When you analyze that, in these six occasions, there are three coming of Jesus Christ, and there are going back, which are the whole mission of Jesus.

Please note that the first coming, second coming, and third coming is not a new doctrine for you to change your religion. Rather, it is a new revelation to wake us up, letting us know there is more truth which is not yet revealed. Therefore, if you believe it or not, it doesn't stop you from going to heaven when He comes back.

The most important thing for you now is to know that Jesus our Lord is coming back soon as we are going to see in this book.

Remarkably, this second coming differs from His first coming as a baby in a manger in the town of Bethlehem surrounded by shepherds. In this second coming, He comes in victory with all authority and supernatural power after overcoming the power of Satan.

Another remarkable point, every occasion of Jesus's different coming and going, there was an angel that came first with a message before Jesus was born, the first, second, and third Coming.

The first angel to Mary mother of Jesus,

The angel went to her and said, "Greetings, you who are highly favored! The Lord is with you." Lk 1:28

The second angel when Jesus was born.

Lk 2:9 An angel of the Lord appeared to them, and the glory of the Lord shone around them, and they were terrified.

The third angel is when He come back from the grave.

Matt 28:–5–6 The angel said to the women, "Do not be afraid, for I know that you are looking for Jesus, who was crucified.6 He is not here; he has risen, just as he said. Come and see the place where he lay.

The angels were always the key messengers to people, like the master of ceremonies giving out the direction of the program.

When Jesus came back for the second time, He said that all authority and power had been given to Him. He came back the second time with a different supernatural body with an aura of heavenly power.

As the scriptures tells us,

> And Jesus came and spoke unto them, saying, all power is given unto me in heaven and in earth. (Matthew 28: 18)

When Jesus's friends found His tomb empty, they knew their master was gone but didn't know where He had gone! It was a confusing moment. But after they saw Him and even touched Him, they all believed what He told them in their fellowship.

When Jesus came back, He lived and moved around for forty days. Jesus proved to the world that He was back as He had promised, and He was alive. He taught His disciples and other followers.

The second coming was very important to His disciples and vitally central to the whole church today. You can imagine if Jesus didn't make it to come back to life! There would be no gospel, and we would have no church today. When He came back to life from the grave, this was indeed the second coming.

This second coming was very important in His mission as the Bible say clearly that:

> But if it is preached that Christ has been raised from the dead, how can some of you say that there is no resurrection of the dead? If there is no resurrection of the dead, then not even Christ has been raised. And if Christ has not been raised, our preaching is useless and so is your faith. More than that, we are then found to be false witnesses about God, for we have testified about God that he raised Christ from the dead. But he did not raise him if in fact the dead are not raised. For if the dead are not raised, then Christ has not been raised either. And if Christ has not been raised, your faith is futile; you are still in your sins. Then those also who have fallen asleep in Christ are lost. If only for this life we have hope in Christ, we are of all people most to be pitied. (1 Corinthians 15:12–19)

Jesus had a big task of convincing His disciples that He was back even though He had talked to them about the program of going and coming back beforehand. Still, it wasn't easy for His disciples to believe Him that this is their Jesus, and He has in fact come back to them. Their own human nature undermined their faith.

The Jesus they were seeing was quite different and mightier than the Jesus they knew before He left them when He died on the cross. Jesus had to show them proof that He was indeed Jesus to the extent of showing them the scars in His hands where the nails had pierced His flesh.

> While they were still talking about this, Jesus himself stood among them and said to them, "Peace be with you." They were startled and

frightened, thinking they saw a ghost. He said to them, "Why are you troubled, and why do doubts rise in your minds? Look at my hands and my feet. It is I myself! Touch me and see; a ghost does not have flesh and bones, as you see I have." (Luke 24:36–39)

This wasn't a simple normal resurrection. No, it was a supernatural of coming back.

As we saw earlier, Jesus in this second coming is of a super nature. It wasn't easy for His disciples to recognize Him, and in fact, it was difficult for anybody to recognize Him. This second part of His mission was to confirm His resurrection as victory and a launchpad to commission His disciples.

5

Jesus's Ministry in His Second Coming (Activity)

This was witnessed by guards, women, and an angel who was sitting on the stone.

The grave of our Lord Jesus Christ was found empty. This was a confirmation that He had defeated death. This heralded His second coming back to the world.

People from different backgrounds made their way to the tomb to make sure that the tomb was really empty. Up to this day, thousands from all corners of the world are still flowing to Jerusalem to look at that same empty tomb. The main activity He had to do was to prove power over death through the resurrection and to commission His disciples. Jesus Christ was in fellowship with His disciples, giving them instructions and taking away their fear and giving them confidence. Jesus was giving them assurance and promising to be with them for all time, giving them guidance and instructions to empower them and giving them direction and mapping out their worldwide mission when He said:

> But ye shall receive power, after that the Holy Ghost comes upon you: and ye shall be witnesses unto me both in Jerusalem, and in all Judaea, and in Samaria, And unto the uttermost part of the earth. (Acts 1:8)

Sending his disciples out to the whole world, they needed God's help and power to carry out the commission they had just been given, starting from Jerusalem to Judea.

> Then he called his twelve disciples together, and gave them power and authority over all devils, and to cure diseases. And he sent them to preach. The kingdom of God, and to heal the sick. (Luke 9:1)

This time, the disciples had a sense of direction; they knew that they had to wait for the Holy Spirit. We can agree about this second coming of Jesus; He had main and specific works and activities for this part of His second coming. The main ministry for Jesus on this second coming was to assure His disciples and all people that He is alive and prove His resurrection—that He is no longer dead, and His body was not stolen but is alive as He had promised.

The second ministry was the commissioning of His disciples. Sending them to go all over the world to tell people what He taught them and to teach the same message to the whole world. On his way going back to His Father, our Lord Jesus had to come back to this world first to commission the apostles to the great ministry. And he was giving his disciple assurance and confirmation on each and every thing and how it is going to work out. Above all, he promised them the most important promise, which is, "I can't leave you like orphans. I'm going to send the Helper, the Holy Spirit, from the Father." He names him as the Helper, so they are sure that they are not alone. They have a comforter—the one to remind them what they were told by their master. "But when the Helper comes, whom shall I send to you from the Father, the Spirit of the truth, who proceeds from the father. He will testify of me."

After proving His resurrection and commissioning His disciples, Jesus was ready to go back to heaven having paid the ransom for mankind to be set free from the shackles of slavery the devil had long dictated upon mankind. He said:

> I came from the Father and entered the world;
> now I am leaving the world and going back to the
> Father. (John 16:28)

An in-depth study of the scriptures uncovers the real story of how Jesus's words were accurately fulfilled.

His first and second coming was fulfilled. We are now waiting for the third coming of our Lord Jesus Christ to take His church. The Lord's return to heaven is to prepare places for you and me and planning His third coming to take His faithful servants. This will be final. Our time now is time for awaiting the third coming. No doubt, we are now waiting for our Lord Jesus to come back for the third time!

> Now when He had spoken these things, while they watched, He was taken up, and a cloud received Him out of their sight. And while they looked steadfastly toward heaven as He went up, behold, two men stood by them in white apparel, who also said, "Men of Galilee, why do you stand

gazing up into heaven? This same Jesus, who was taken up from you into heaven, will so come in like manner as you saw Him go into heaven." (Acts 1:9–11)

We can see again the angels coming back with a message as Jesus was taken away, like the angels appearing on different occasions with a message regarding what was taking place.

6

Now We Are Waiting for Our Lord Jesus to Come Back for the Third Time

It is true for someone to say that the church has been behind the clock or behind the time. It is for this sad reason that many are waiting for our Lord to come for the second time when actually the Second Coming took place on earth two thousand years ago. We are now waiting for Him to come back for the third time as the final coming.

It is very important to have a revelation and knowledge of His coming before we understand the whole mission of our Lord Jesus, how it started and how He is going to end up His mission according to the word of God. Failure to recognize the above facts would be disastrous. The Jews who saw Jesus for a third of a century doubted to the end and revealed cases of classic confusion until the day He ascended to heaven.

As it is written in the Book of Acts,

> Now when He had spoken these things, while they watched, He was taken up, and a cloud received Him out of their sight. And while they looked steadfastly toward heaven as He went up, behold, two men stood by them in white apparel, who also said, "Men of Galilee, why do you stand gazing up into heaven? This *same* Jesus, who was taken up

from you into heaven, will so come in like manner
as you saw Him go into heaven." (Acts 1:9–11)

As you read this book, the Spirit of God is going to give you more revelation of His whole mission and how He is going to come back soon. We will then know that this is the third coming of Jesus Christ since we have seen the ministries and activities of Jesus on His first and second coming.

We need to know the undertakings and activities of our Lord Jesus that He has to accomplish when He comes for His third coming. These are the harbingers of His return. Then we will understand how soon He will come for His final mission. Our Lord has gone back to heaven to meet His heavenly Father after the accomplishment of the first two parts of His earthly mission. He was taken to heaven before their eyes. The Angels prophesied the coming back of Jesus Christ to His disciples.

"Which also said, ye men of Galilee, why stand ye gazing up into heaven? This same Jesus, who is taken up from you into heaven, shall so come in like manner as ye have seen him go into heaven."

These angels wanted their message to be clear to the disciples when they said "same way they saw Him" coming in the first coming is the same way they saw him on the second coming and the same way will see him coming in the third coming.

The angels asking this question to these men tells us the angels knew the time and season of what was going on at that time. The truth is that His third coming will not be a secret, and as the Word of God says: "Every eye shall see Him. None of His comings was secret; every occasion of each part of His coming was prophesied before it happened, therefore there was no secret."

When Jesus came first into the world on His mission, His first coming was not a secret. His dying on the cross was not a secret, His second coming back from the world of the dead was not a secret, and His coming back for the third time will not be a secret either. We know what we are waiting for, and when the time comes as the Bible says, it will not be a secret. The Bible says that every eye will see Him.

That is why, whether you believe in His coming back or not, it does not change anything. He is coming back. Not everybody believed in His first coming to be born. And He was born.

The Bible tells us, "No one knows the day and hour." It's true, but when that day comes, that hour will no longer be a secret at all.

And when the time came for Him to come back to life, not everybody believed Him, but He came back to life. Today, you have a choice to make because the time is coming when you will have no choice but to obey.

It is written: "As surely as I live," says the Lord, "Every knee will bow before me; every tongue will acknowledge God." (Romans 14:11)

In the same way, He is coming back for the third time. The doubters shall doubt. Please don't doubt; He is coming back! Like the singer proclaims, when the roll is called up yonder make sure you are there!

Even if it looks as if He has delayed, still He is coming back; nothing will stop Him from coming back as He has promised. Like a long night in the forest looks so permanent so is the waiting; finally, it dawns, and the sun comes through the blankets of dark grey clouds of forgotten years. We will be waiting albeit as men of very little faith. The assured voice of the Bible rings through to announce as it is written in the book of Hebrews:

> For in just a very little while, He who is coming
> will come and will not delay. (Hebrews 10:37)

As of old, the Lord is keeping His word. As it was in His first and second coming, the voice still calls from the desert to wake up the saints from our empty slumbering nations.

> Look, I'm coming soon! Blessed is the one who keeps the words of the prophecy written in this scroll. (Revelation 22:7)

As the Word of God tells us that his Word never goes out and comes back void, it is the same way his coming is at hand.

The inquisitive world has perpetuated the seemingly answerless questions. The importance of the first coming is still hazy in the eyes of the inhabitants of this world while the second coming is simply looked at as merely another occurrence among a multitude of events that have come and gone by.

7

Why Jesus Has to Come Back for the Third Time

The impasse above calls for answers to the next big question: Why should Jesus come back for the third time, and why is He coming back into this world again, especially since the world is even more evil than ever before?

We are going to see in the scriptures and the words of Jesus Christ prophesying about His coming back to us physically.

There are several reasons behind His coming back to this earth, but some of the main reasons are summarized in one sentence: He has to accomplish the whole mission which was given to Him by His Father in heaven and, majorly to keep his word, to judge the living and the dead of His church and for the Father to glorify His Son. Both Matthew the evangelist and Isaiah the prophet attest to this long ignored reality.

> Heaven and earth will pass away, But my words will not pass away. (Matt 24:35)

> So is my word that goes out from my mouth: It will not return to me empty but will accomplish what I desire and achieve the purpose for which I sent it. (Isaiah 55:11)

His coming is justified. The third coming is something we cannot ignore nor just explain away. He promised to come back; therefore, He has to do it in order to bring fulfillment to what He said He would do.

With His third coming, the universe will witness two examples of judgment. He is coming with reward and punishment. Each will take what he deserves and what he worked for. At this time, Jesus is not coming as Savior, for that is a deal already done. Jesus is coming as both a judge and as a reward giver.

> Look, I am coming soon! My reward is with me,
> and I will give to each person according to what
> they have done. (Revelation 22:12)

This scripture shows us that Jesus knows everybody; He knows our works and knows whatever each one of us deserves. To one will be judgment and a sentence while to another, it will be time to stand up, be counted, and triumphantly given a priceless crown of glory. Happy are those who like the Apostle Paul will thus give the ultimate testimony:

> I have fought a good fight. I have run the race.
> I have kept the faith. Finally there is laid up for
> me a crown of righteousness which the Lord,
> the righteous judge, will give to me on that day.
> (Timothy 4:7–8)

The only redeeming feature on that awesome day of the Lord is that even the saint called Paul knows that he will not be alone. The selfless man of God remembers other people that will be crowned on that day. They are you and I who zealously await the Lord's coming. It is good and befitting to say halleluiah again and again.

> Now there is in store for me the crown of righteousness, which the Lord, the righteous Judge,

will award to me on that day—and not only to me, but also to all who have longed for his appearing. (2 Timothy 4:8, NIV)

Paul in his letter to Timothy was trying to say to him and to us, "Join me, because nobody has to miss this moment." It's true. It's free to everybody. There is no good reason to miss it.

This means they are people who will be ready for their reward on the spot as per His Word. But when scripture talks about reward and its opposite according to what we have done, that means there is another side for those who are not going to get a reward but judgment. The judgments will be fair indeed as this will be done by the fairest of them all. There is no excuse for the world to straying from the path of righteousness, for we serve the same God who decreed that:

> For I the Lord your God am a jealous God, visiting the iniquity of the fathers upon the children to the third and fourth generation of those that hate me. (Genesis 20:5)

It will be a great day indeed because on that same day, some will be receiving their reward, and others will be sent before the wedding party starts as per Jesus's words. As the proverb goes, "Forewarned is forearmed." Therefore, what is written in Scripture will come to pass as we find it in the book of *Matthew*.

> Many will say to me on that day, "Lord, Lord, did we not prophesy in your name and in your name drive out demons and in your name perform many miracles?" Then I will tell them plainly, "I never knew you. Away from me, you evildoers!" (Matthew 7:22–23, NIV)

Nobody would like to hear this statement in his life, but this still will happen—to some of our friends, relatives, but it's not too late for you to come out from these people to be left out.

It is time we look at who these people that Jesus is talking about are when He says that He will tell them plainly that He never knew them. Who exactly will He be talking to?

Most world preachers don't normally preach or teach about these truth verses. It is time we believe that it is to us that Jesus will say His word vividly and plainly! Jesus will talk to us openly! This still looks bearable; there is still another category that will summarily get marching orders there and then.

Let the words in this book be a trumpet in your spirit and wisdom to your heart or let them be like a wake-up call when you have a very serious and very important morning appointment. Because when you wake up on the morning everything you do or any time you have that morning is controlled by the important appointment, for one reason you don't want to miss the appointment. The same way don't miss his coming.

8

Jesus Will Deny Some People (I Don't Know You!)

For Jesus to say the above to you is a disaster of immense proportions. It is like a pilot ordering a passenger to leave the plane when it is airborne. It is disheartening to learn that Jesus will deny some people when all of us, though from different backgrounds, believe in Jesus as our savior. The sad reality is that there will be some who will be denied by Jesus himself! A thing so lamentable indeed!

It seems confusing to most people. The giant question is deafening: Who are these people Jesus is talking about? This is so scary, especially when the Scriptures say that Jesus will deny people who shouted His name routinely on a daily basis.

Then we ask ourselves about who are using His name? A simple analysis about which Christians fit the bill reveals that they must be those who use His name in their line of duty.

Needless to say, they must be some believers and some ministers of the gospel from different backgrounds whose trade is to preach the gospel. They naturally have the name of Jesus planted on their lips! It will be a shocking moment indeed when the judge is condemned, and the prosecutor becomes the criminal who has contravened the laws He was supposed to defend.

What will it be like when Jesus comes back, and you hear from Him candidly that He doesn't know you! Come to think about it; it will be appalling and too depressing to hear, but it's true. Some will hear that statement, and it will be openly said and certainly final.

In this book, we have to talk about this issue because it is very serious though confusing. Since Jesus is coming soon, we need to know and understand to do something quickly. We don't want to be taken by surprise or be caught unaware. This will be a shocking moment to many people who don't expect to hear such statement from the Christ, who they thought to be their savior and Lord.

Apostle Paul talked about it when he said that he didn't want to lose it after ministering to others.

> No, I strike a blow to my body and make it my slave so that after I have preached to others, I myself will not be disqualified for the prize. (1 Corinthians 9:27)

As the apostle Paul looked into this matter, in his words, he means that it's possible to serve and be left out at the same time. This means there is a possibility after all you have done which everybody can see and praise you and then be left out. That would be very sad.

My friend, are you a renowned miracle worker or a renowned prophet or a popular minister in any way? This is specifically for us who are using His name. This scripture is direct to those who are ministers in different ministries doing everything using His name, Jesus's name, from all different religious backgrounds.

Let us look at the truth in the Word of God, which is tangible, and these are some of the main points and facts: Consider when He said that whatever you ask Him in His Name, He will do it so that the Father may be glorified in the Son. What this scripture means is whatever Jesus himself is doing in His name is to glorify his Father.

That means that whatever is done by Jesus and those that purport to support Him is to glorify the heavenly Father but not for personal glory.

While sharing this truth with His disciples, Jesus talked about what He was doing and how He conducted His ministries. He said:

> For I came down from heaven, not to do mine own will, but the will of him that sent me. (John 6:38)

Our Lord Jesus is very clear by saying even if He came direct from heaven, He didn't have to create His own style of teaching or His own words, not even doing what He personally wanted. Everything was about the plan's originator who is the heavenly Father.

Apostle Paul was following his Master's words when he said,

> Let me tell you, my friends, that the gospel I preach is not of human origin. I did not receive it from any human being, nor did anyone teach it to me. It was Jesus Christ himself who revealed it to me. (Galatians 1:11–12)

Paul is emphasizing the fact that the gospel he preaches originates from our Lord Jesus Christ which Jesus said He got from His heavenly Father.

There are some questions a minister needs to ask himself. The main question should be about whether what you are doing in your ministry is indeed in His name. The other question is whether indeed you were called by Him and are doing what He directed you to do? On the other hand, you could be doing your own thing and just using His name as a point of reference.

Remember, Jesus said,

> I'm going to the father, but I promise to be with
> you as long as you are doing what I send you to
> do. I will be with you always. It's a promise.

That means that even before His coming back the third time,
He is around us, watching you and me, seeing how we are doing His
work and how we are using His name.

> Teaching them to observe all I have commanded
> you. And behold I'm with you always to the end
> of the age. (Matt 28:20)

Jesus Christ is observing and monitoring our work as we are
serving Him daily in His name. Today, I don't know how many times
He has visited you. But let us ask ourselves: Are we still on the original gospel from our Lord Jesus, the original gospel blessed by his
heavenly Father? What the Scriptures say is true: that some preach
about Christ because they are jealous, bitter, and some have different
interests.

> It is true that some preach Christ out of envy and
> rivalry, but others out of goodwill. The latter do
> so out of love, knowing that I am put here for the
> defense of the gospel. The former preach Christ
> out of selfish ambition, not sincerely, supposing
> that they can stir up trouble for me while I am
> in chains. But what does it matter? The import-
> ant thing is that in every way, whether from false
> motives or true, Christ is preached. And because
> of this I rejoice. (Philippians 1:15–18)

Some other preachers teach about Christ because they have
other interests. Apostle Paul says that the important thing is that the
gospel is being preached even though some preach for their own fame
and other interests but still the gospel is preached. Can we imagine
the fact that Jesus is patiently watching preachers use His name in

vain while they work for their own prosperity? We use the name and take His glory to ourselves. This is both unfair and suicidal. Can we sincerely ask ourselves today why we are doing what we are doing? The true answer to that question is deep in our hearts. In most cases, in everything we do in each one and everybody's heart, they must be the real truth inside your heart because you can't hide your truth from your heart.

9

Jesus Is with Us, Observing and Monitoring

This is His vineyard. The Lord is following closely what the workers are actually doing. Our Lord Jesus promised to be around us as we serve Him. Jesus promised to be with us as we serve Him. He empowers and inspires us but also observes and monitors our work as we serve Him. This goes deeper when He comes and visits us in our homes, in our offices, and in our ministries. It is for this reason that He says that He was hungry, and you gave Him food; He was thirsty, and you gave Him drink. He was a stranger, and you welcomed Him.

> For I was hungry, and you gave me something to eat; I was thirsty, and you gave me something to drink. I was a stranger, and you invited me in. I needed clothes, and you clothed me. I was sick, and you looked after me; I was in prison, and you came to visit me. Then the righteous will answer him, "Lord, when did we see you hungry and feed you, or thirsty and give you something to drink? When did we see you a stranger and invite you in, or needing clothes and clothe you? When did we see you sick or in prison and go to visit you?" The King will reply, "Truly I tell you, whatever you did for one of the least of these

brothers and sisters of mine, you did for me."
(Matthew 25:35–39)

This will be another shocking statement from Jesus when He comes back. After knowing the truth from Him, that He has been with us daily in our day-to-day life, stop thinking that you are on your own and should do whatever you want. Like the song in my school days goes:

> They are watching you,
> Marking all you do,
> Hearing the things that you say,
> Let them the Savior as He shines in you,
> Let His power control you every day!

That is a childhood song, but it presents a true picture of what is actually reality. Do you know sometimes Jesus has been coming to us with thirst asking for water, but instead of giving Him water, we made Him (for seed) pay for the water in Jesus's name; we also ask him to pay for healing when He is actually the healer? Think about it: Jesus Christ buying a blessing and water from you in Jesus's name! Because Jesus himself keeps coming in and out as he promised, and we don't notice him. If you remember the story, "On the Road to Emmaus" in Luke 24:13 after Jesus's resurrection, which says,

> Two of them were going to a village called Emmaus, about seven miles[a] from Jerusalem. They were talking with each other about everything that had happened. As usually people talk about the new or what has happened in their city or neighborhood the same way these men as they talked and discussed these things with each other, Jesus himself came up and walked along with them; but they were kept from recognizing him. the same way is coming to your daily activities and keeps coming in normal fellowship.

He asked them, "What are you discussing together as you walk along?"

They stood still, their faces downcast. One of them, named Cleopas, asked him, "Are you the only one visiting Jerusalem who does not know the things that have happened there in these days?" Mr. Cleopas was asking Jesus what happen to a man called Jesus.

"What things?" he asked. Thank God these men they didn't ask him something to answer his questions

"About Jesus of Nazareth," they replied. Note this they are telling Jesus a story about Jesus "He was a prophet, powerful in word and deed before God and all the people. The chief priests and our rulers handed him over to be sentenced to death, and they crucified him; but we had hoped that he was the one who was going to redeem Israel. And what is more, it is the third day since all this took place. In addition, some of our women amazed us. They went to the tomb early this morning.

You can imagine how many times Jesus has come to your kingdom, to your office, in your personal life, or in your discussion, and you don't recognize him.

As you read this book, ask yourself from inside your heart—why are you doing what you are doing in His name? Don't you think one day, you may ask Him also to pay for His own grace.

When did I see you, Jesus, coming to my office? You will be surprised by the way you treated Him when He visited you. He is around us whenever we are busy doing anything in our ministry in His name. On some occasions, Jesus asks for an appointment to see you, man/woman of God, but unfortunately, you are too busy or have no time or ask for some amount from Him to see you.

This is happening everywhere. People are preaching in their own style for their own sake. Have you ever heard of a preacher asking for a big amount of money in exchange for a big healing or a big blessing? Sometimes they have in fact asked Jesus Christ to pay for blessing in the name of Jesus! This is extremely sad. My beloved, our Lord Jesus is watching you doing all this in His name. Can you now give a reason why Jesus should not deny you?

There is nowhere in Scripture that Jesus ever asked for any payment for Him to do any healing or from anybody to receive a blessing. Gifts are good, and there is nothing wrong to teach about seed gifts, and giving is good and biblical. Giving is better than receiving; it's true. But the way we use it distorts the truth of the gospel of our Lord Jesus. Our Lord Jesus is coming back soon. But before He shows up, He is around us watching and observing how we are doing His work in our ministries and in our churches. That is the reason you have this book in your hands as a trumpet to wake you up from the good works you have been doing. You have to take more seriousness and more sensitive how treat people and how we handle each and every person who comes to you. The more you take the Word of God seriously, the more you increase your obedience.

The same way it happens to King Saul. He wasn't sensitive to the word of the prophet from God.

Remember 1 Samuel 15:8–9, King Saul was told to destroy all Amalekites. King Saul had heard the word very clearly from God; he knew what he was supposed to do but because of the people around King Saul, he didn't do the way he was told to do by his God. He substituted God's advice for man's lies. Saul lost it that day:

> I greatly regret that I have set up Saul as king
> for he has turned back from Me, and has not

performed My commandments, and it grieved
Samuel, and he cried out to the Lord all night.
(1Samuel 15:11)

Being called and being gifted is the work of the Holy Spirit, but
how you use them for doing the works of the One who called you
and gifted you is your responsibility for which you will be given a
prize or a rebuke from the One who sent you. At the end of the story,
the Lord God regretted why He made Saul a King. As you read this
book, can you account for how many people are surrounding you?

The world we live in is indeed a complex one. Men and women
who are around you are more fans and cheerers than true recipients
of the word; the "fans" send and will force you to say what they want
to hear. They will shower you with praise and give you titles that
belong to someone else. In such times of frenzy, they address you
as king, prophet, apostle, mighty, and even Lord. To compound the
tragedy, you will declare yourself a healer, a crasher of all demons,
a healer of all diseases, and even promise to bring the dead to life.
Derailed from the track of your calling, the referee will indeed find
you offside. When the true Redeemer comes, most of us will look
fake indeed. Listen, they are destroying you and killing you spiritually. The sheep are killing the shepherd!

You are working hard doing what pleases men and everybody
around you, but your Lord and God may be wondering, *why you are
doing what you are doing in His name?*

The merciful Jesus's word is not worried about what you are
doing with His name; the gospel is preached regardless of your personal interest. Nevertheless, be aware the Lord has already decided: "I
will speak out publicly. I don't know you," He has said.

It is not too late! Please stop and have a break to look into your
heart, your personal life, and your ministry, and look at Him with
the eyes of your soul before He physically appears in the sky. Seek

Him and find out yourself, where you are today with Him? Are you still in good books with him? Does He know you? Maybe you are well known on TV stations or radio stations, or well known, highly respected and accepted by all men. All this means nothing if you can't abide in the truth of Jesus's words.

Don't be taken by the excitement around your seat of *honors* or what people around you say about you. We see King Saul was rejected as King by God who had made him a king because he focused on what was around him and heeded the advice given by those around him instead of God who had anointed him to be a king.

Here is one example which is a true story, This happened to me:

One day, I lost my Visa card, and it took me some days before recovering my missing card. That card had been authorized by the bank to enable me to transact business. My name was on it, and I could buy anything using the same card.

It had the power to do anything in my name in terms of buying and paying for anything. Unfortunately, the one who picked it up started using the card to buy whatever he wanted in my name. The card had no problem and could perform its duties as it was authorized by the bank in my name to do.

So my Visa card was out there performing miracles and wonders, and the one who was using it received many appreciations and praises for being a good customer. After a few days, I discovered that my card was missing and went straight to my bank to stop it.

At the bank, I found a bank official who printed out for me the history of my account. I found out that there were two pages of transactions of purchases from my card which had been performed.

The bank official asked me, 'Sir, did you do all these payments?"

"No," I said.

Then she asked me whether I knew who did all this in my name with my card? I said that I didn't know him or her.

From that day, the scripture from Matthew 7:23 got double meaning and understanding to me. I understood what Jesus meant when he said, "Get away from me, wicked people. I don't know you."

It is possible that there are very many people today who are using His name when He doesn't know them. Just like the wicked person who used my card. There are two different parts: part one, the name of Jesus has power to do everything; part two is that the one who uses the name of Jesus totally may be a different person.

Again, like the wicked person who used my card, always remember this truth: wherever you move with God's gift or God's power, it is not yours, and it is not about you, and it is not to serve your personal interest; it is about Him.

Everything done in His name, it's about His Father's glory, and when you know the truth, you must do it.

You are His son and servant; that is the reason Jesus will say, "Thank you, my faithful servant." And don't forget, as you read this book, I just want to remind you that Jesus Christ our Lord is coming back soon. Therefore, please don't be among those who will be caught by surprises.

Take a moment always to check your heart in your private time for your private life because there is always truth within your heart and with God. You have to know this is true. Where nobody can see or know what a friend, your wife, or your husband cannot know about you, it is known by God; and it is written that He sees the nakedness of our heart.

Behold, you delight in truth in the inward being,
and you teach me wisdom in the secret heart.
(Psalm 51:6)

You can face your truth within your heart as you read this book. The Spirit of the Lord will minister to you and save you from the confusion brought by the devil. There are many different evil spirits operating in the world today that are ready to confuse the church.

There is a multitude of evil spirits which are operating in our countries and our ministries; they are operating in high places, and you will find out some mentioned here are operating around you. These are the spirit of confusion, spirits of deceitfulness, the spirit of pride, the spirit of false teaching, the spirit of false prophecy, the spirit of immorality, the spirit of fighting each other—fighting for identity and fame, spirit of greed, the spirit of duplication, the spirit of depression and operation, the spirit of computation, and more evil from the den of the devil. These are moving around and working hard to take you away the reward you got from Jesus and kept for you.

In this book, we are not going to talk in detail about how these evil spirits operate. Next time, we will be talking about how these evil spirits are busy operating around the body of Christ.

10

Who Are These People Jesus Is coming Back For?

There are many believers who believe today in Jesus Christ but have a different opinion about who is going to heaven and who is not going to heaven.

In this book, we will not be judging anybody like some people do: judging others based on what they believe; we would like to start from the question what Jesus himself said about those people He is coming back for himself.

He is coming back as He said,

> Do not let your hearts be troubled. You believe in God; believe also in me. My Father's house has many rooms; if that were not so, would I have told you that I am going there to prepare a place for you? And if I go and prepare a place for you, I will come back and take you to be with me that you also may be where I am. (John 14:1–3)

Jesus Christ emphasized the point of not being troubled because He knew in this time of His coming, there will be a lot of messiness and confusion, fear, different problems, and many will be troubled with all these confusions which are happening today. So we should not be troubled when we find ourselves in this situation; instead, we should believe in Him. The most important thing is not to be troubled by anything.

We must believe in God and believe in Jesus. By believing in God, it means believing that He is coming for you. Because He is not coming for your group, He is not coming for a big church building, a big congregation, not a specific denomination as many people think, not the most popular church, and not the church with the biggest budget. He is not coming for Black churches or White churches, not at all. He is coming back to take you personally.

All these mentioned above are small hideouts where we hide and take cover to justify ourselves and reconcile in our hearts with God's business in our daily life.

In our places today, we have big titles in churches and ministries. Sometimes, we grade ourselves and others based on their educational qualifications like doctors, apostles, and bishops while others of us are called lords, or high level titles of theologians, etc. Brethren, all are good but, my friend, none of these is among Jesus's criteria for the choice of the church He is coming to take as we find out in scriptures.

With Jesus's word, He will never say, "Well done, my doctor or my chief apostle or prophet." But He will say, "Well done, my *faithful servant.*"

Jesus continues to insist about personalizing the reward, which means personal relationship.

> Look, I am coming soon! My reward is with me, and I will give to each person according to what they have done. (Revelation 22:12)

This is Jesus's word saying I'm coming soon; yes, He is coming and is coming with a reward, and that reward is for *each person*. Note that His reward is not for your specific group nor even for a specific denomination. This reward Jesus is coming with is for each one of us.

The reward is for you and personal, and it's very clear it's according to what you have done. That means our rewards are not the same because each one of us did his or her work differently.

Normally, someone who gives out a reward must know the person he is giving the reward to, and he must know what he did to deserve the reward. That is how much our Lord Jesus Christ knows each one of us. Please, don't hide in any crowd or group of people or religion; this is about you. We will not have any excuse. We won't be like King Saul who gave God's people an excuse of his own failures. We need not be like the sick man at the pool of Siloam—the man who was waiting for healing.

> One who was there had been an invalid for thirty-eight years. When Jesus saw him lying there and learned that he had been in this condition for a long time, he asked him, "Do you want to get well?"
>
> "Sir," the invalid replied, "I have no one to help me into the pool when the water is stirred. While I am trying to get in, someone else goes down ahead of me."
>
> Then Jesus said to him, "Get up! Pick up your mat and walk." (John 5:5–8)

This man was in a bad condition for thirty-eight years with a lot of excuses. By talking about pinpointing others like angels came by, and the water stirred, like no one was there to help me; instead, point out the other people that went down before me. Jesus asked this man to simply do what was right and stop all these excuses. What about you, and what about me? Do you want to get well?

My friend, at this time, we should stop giving excuses. I don't know how long you have been in that condition or that same situation you are going through. Jesus said I'm coming soon; do you want to get My reward? Then get up or pick yourself up and move forward. Our denominations are good for helping us to see the way, but we have to move forward, and we need to be focused in a true way on Jesus Christ. Religion is not to blame for the religious chaos of our time. Our religions and denominations are good for helping us to point and show us the way to heaven, like the signpost in the junction of the road that shows you the way, where it says, "TO THE SAND BEACH" and sign point to the direction that takes you to the sand beach. But the truth is that signpost has never been to sand beach, and it will never go to sand beach. Therefore, after reading the signpost, you don't stop and stand on the signpost. What you'll do is to thank God and whoever put the signpost with the assurance and go to sand beach. The same way, thank God for your denomination and your religion and go ahead.

> Whatever you do, work at it with all your heart, as working for the Lord, not for human masters since you know that you will receive an inheritance from the Lord as a reward. It is the Lord Christ you are serving. Anyone who does wrong will be repaid for their wrongs, and there is no favoritism. (Colossians 3:23–25)

We need to know that serving God is a privilege. It is only God's work that has a remuneration which will remain forever. When He comes, some people will regret for one thing: they had a lot of privilege and opportunity to serve Him and did not use it.

The Word of God is very clear about which church is coming to give a reward and take it. That church is an individual person and that person is you.

This is your personal issue. This is personal relationship with Him.

It's time to stop looking outside yourself and start looking at yourself from inside of yourself to outside and see your personal relationship with Him without comparing yourself with others or anything around you.

> Look, he is coming with the clouds,_and every eye will see him, even those who pierced him; and all peoples on earth will mourn because of him._So shall it be! Amen. "I am the Alpha and the Omega," says the Lord God, "who is, and who was, and who is to come, the Almighty." (Revelation 1:7–8)

The Scripture says that every eye shall see Him. That means that there will be no secrets. But for the reward, the Scriptures say again *each person* according to what he or she has done; this is for all Christians from every Christian background believing in Jesus Christ.

If you have a living Christ inside you, no matter where you are praying from, having a living Christ in you and having a personal relationship with Jesus Christ, you are the main reason why Jesus Christ is coming back the third time to this world. You are the church and temple of the Holy Spirit.

> Don't you know that you yourselves are God's temple and that God's Spirit dwells in your midst? If anyone destroys God's temple, God will destroy that person; for God's temple is sacred, and you together are that temple. (1 Corinthians 3:16–17)

It is the same in His sight if you are from the church that sits under a tree and has no building and has no good seats or if you are from the church that is in a big building and has marble, wall to wall carpet, and is expensively built. It is the same thing if maybe you come from a very important denomination or from some denomination that is not known.

All these are good, but He is not coming back for any of these. You are personally the most important individual Jesus is coming for. Our Lord Jesus Christ is very clear, and there are very important words He said when He talked about His coming back for the third time. This is very important to you too. Jesus said,

> I am coming soon. Hold on to what you have, so that no one will take your crown. (Revelation 3:11)

We all know that a crown goes on one head not two and not three. This means one person, one crown. Above all, before you hold onto anything, you must know what you have before you hold onto it. By knowing the value of what you have, it will inspire you to hold onto it strongly. Therefore, knowing what you have and knowing the value of what you have in Christ will force you to strongly hold onto it.

Today, some have exchanged what they have in Christ for fame, popularity, and wealth. They know Jesus has taken long to come back, and many thought He has gone for good.

What we all are seeing today in church or in the body of Christianity is as if everybody has forgotten about the words of Jesus when he said, "I'm coming back." Jesus Christ stands on His word when He says, "I'm coming soon."

It is good to spare a moment and ask ourselves these pertinent questions:

Do I know what I have in Christ or what I have to hold on to? What is the value of what I have in Christ?

Knowing the value motivates you to keep it safe; after knowing the value of his debit card or credit card in his money pocket (wallet), he or she will keep it very close. The person will keep the card safe according to the value it has for him.

I mean real protection, no jokes. It will be his pocket where he keeps his *Visa/MasterCard* because he knows the value.

The most important thing is, when Jesus talked about holding onto what you have, He didn't mean to hold onto the materials or property you have nor your prosperity, not even your popularity. Not the value of bank accounts, but the value I have in Christ and my relationship with Him.

What you have in Christ Jesus is the salvation inside you which was paid by the price of the blood of Jesus Christ. Nobody can take it away from you when you know and understand what Jesus Christ was talking about "holding onto what you have." Keep what you have, which was given to you, when you accepted Jesus Christ as your personal savior. The salvation you received is Christ in you; please keep Him, and hold on. There is no price which can compensate with price of the blood of Jesus.

Jesus insisted by saying,

> Look, I am coming soon! Blessed is the one who keeps the words of the prophecy written in this scroll. (Revelation 22:7)

My friends, don't look for the blessings elsewhere; you will be blessed by keeping the words of God. Don't give opportunity to the false prophets and false teachers with evil spirits to take advantage of you. You are looking for blessings in the wrong place. You have all blessings by obeying and keeping the Word of God.

Today, the gospel of blessing is very popular because people are desperate because they are missing their personal relationship with God who blesses freely. Today, people say they believe in being children of God, but we are busy vainly chasing everywhere looking for blessings.

But God loves you so much that He gave His only son to die for you and His Son Jesus Christ who loves you so much that He is coming back for you. You can't miss any blessing He has planned for you. What He has done to you already is more powerful than any blessing you could ever want from the world.

Then Jesus went back to be with His Father in heaven. He left with us a promise of coming back, and His coming back is at hand and closer than what we can imagine. That is why the trumpet of His coming is all over—waking us up to be awake and wait with a sense of not being left out.

11

The World Is Changing with All Its Involvement as We Are Waiting for Our Lord Jesus

Changes are taking place daily all over the world in each and every sector of our lives. We witness climate change, technological change, moral behavior changes, and human character is changing in every nation worldwide. God is the best designer when He designed the best super natural creation infrastructure of the universe. The way He organized the water and separating it from land, well-organized obiter in space, He did everything well organized and perfect to benefit human being. Unfortunately, what God had organized for human being, as they are the beneficiary, instead they have contributed in disorganizing the God's order He set for them. It's like when you organize your house and somebody comes in and disorganize what you organized. When you find that person is busy disorganizing your house and you ask him to fix it back to your order, he will not be able to fix it back the way you did it because he doesn't know how you did it. This climate change and environment problem is one of physical signs of the coming back of our Lord Jesus.

Today, we have what they call climate change, which has caused a lot of big distractions and loss of people's life. This climate change is not just changing its climate destruction, it's a big issue but people try to use easy and simple words. It's not easy and simple as they think because the campaigning from worldwide nations and big organization and big country (super power nation) have tried to stop and trying to do something about the climate change but nothing come out instead it is becoming worse and worse.

When the destruction takes place from climate change like wildfire, huge storms, tsunami, floods, tornadoes, typhoons, and many others, they call them natural disaster or mother nature just because nobody has the technology or any power to stop it. They keep talking emotionally about climate change and predicate how is becoming too bad and critical condition in future, but it keeps going on worse to worse. This is another big challenge the world is facing and it has no power to control.

As days going on, we are going to experience worldwide more and bigger destructions from climate change. This is going to be happening in different parts of the world. More destruction of wildfires, more destruction from different strong storms, more floods, and huge volcano eruptions. When you see this happening, just remember that is one of the sign of the trumpet of His coming.

All these changes indicate the signs of the end of the world. As you read this book based on the Word of God, you will find out that all signs and all prophesy of the end of the world have already taken place while others are taking place today in our villages, towns, and cities. It is happening before our eyes!

These days, we are moving and living in the last days of the coming of our Lord Jesus Christ. Because His coming is too close, many foretold events are taking place.

> For false Christ's and false prophets will arise and perform great signs and wonders, so as to lead astray, if possible, even the elect. (Matthew 24:24)

The antichrist spirit is moving and operating around our towns, cities, and villages. In some countries today, the church is going through persecution more than ever before. What the Word of God said about in those days, we can see today.

> Then they will deliver you up to tribulation and put you to death, and you will be hated by all nations for my name's sake. And then many will fall away and betray one another and hate one another. And many false prophets will arise and lead many astray. And because lawlessness will be increased, the love of many will grow cold. (Matthew 24:9–12)

Persecution is taking place in many different nations. Notably, this spirit of the antichrist doesn't only fight Christianity but is also exchanging Christ's truth with counterfeits. These changes are happening dangerously fast. They are at a terrific speed. It is the reason why most times, we miss to know or take notes of what is going on. The speed is too high, and the whole saga leaves us perplexed!

As a church, we need to wake up so that we may not be taken by surprise. Many today are being taken unaware by the changes without even noticing what is going on around them, for there is an information explosion; changes are recklessly happening, and everything seems to be moving extremely fast.

Among these many changes and signs, we are going to mention only few. If you read the Word of God, you will notice that the evil has already covered the world in different ways.

As we see, what is blatantly evil has become more popular, and it has come out to the pulpit and the altar just as the Bible predicted. As the Word of God says when you see the evil come out:

> Because of the increase of wickedness, the love of most will grow cold, but the one who stands firm to the end will be saved. And this gospel of the kingdom will be preached in the whole world

as a testimony to all nations, and then the end
will come. So when you see standing in the holy
place "the abomination that causes desolation,"
spoken of through the prophet Daniel, let the
reader understand. (Matthew 24:12–15)

According to this word of God, if you can agree with me, this is
already happening, where most of the evil which the Bible is calling
abomination to be standing in the pulpit, altar, or holy place is with
us in these days. Today, in our cities, evil is being practiced in the
pulpit and on altars in many areas. The old tent had an altar where
they would give God sacrifices or a pulpit in church to minister, but
today we have a stage in church where anybody can stand and act to
entertain people with different kinds of drama like an action movie.

As it is written, nothing was hidden in secret which will not be
revealed. Evil is no longer done in secret, it's done openly, and the
evildoer has no more shame. Sin is now normal. Any evil or shameful
act that used to be in secret is done openly today, and it's normal.
Most of it is legalized by states and nations. Very scary indeed! Today,
the evil and sin is being given a special permit by the government.
The weapon of high authorities use is the word "law." Simply, the
word law has legalized this evil. You can imagine.

Remember Jesus on the cross. He died and resurrected and
overcome the power of law and sin. That is the reason the weak forces
are still fighting for the law and sin.

That is why we hear people telling you it is legal to do such evil.
It is no longer a sin; it is accepted by the law. That is one of the ways
the evil spirits are operating in high places.

The reason why these changes are so fast and influence the
whole word is simple to see. The devil and his demons are very much
aware that the coming back of our Lord Jesus is very soon. The devil

is feeling the heat of His coming, and day by day, the temperature is rising higher and higher.

The only thing Satan and his forces have to do is to enrich more different forged styles and immoralities into the world and everybody's lifestyle. It is also affecting the church as the body of Christ.

The most confusing part is that the Christians who have the power of Christ as He promised them, instead of standing in that power to resist the devil, they support counterfeit lies of the devil, and they end up taken in by these changes without noticing what is actually happening.

Satan and his demons are taking advantage of so-called technology to propagate his counterfeit gospel. We are calling them new arrivals, new style, new development, but we don't know where these new arrivals are coming from or where these new changes are coming from, and where they are taking us as church. Jesus said in His word He is the same today, yesterday, and doesn't change, and His message never changes.

Do you know that many Bible verses were removed from the Bible on your iPad or on your phone? The removed verses are the main key verses of salvation. Meaning, whoever is doing these attacks on the Word of God knows what he is doing. These are new changes that have attacked the Word of God and at the same time attacked the children of God.

New changes that come with technology have gone too far to change God's Word. Besides removing the verses from the Bible, the same technology spreads evil worldwide. However, we have a warning to everyone who will change by removing or adding on to what God gave us: that they will be in serious trouble.

I warn everyone who hears the words of the prophecy of this scroll: If anyone adds anything to them, God will add to that person the plagues described in this scroll. (Revelation 22:18)

The same technology is being used. Just let us look at our normal phone. The technology on your handset phone today is in charge of your life; it has destroyed the natural human attitude and character. The phone has divided families where you find nobody thinks about another in the house as everybody is busy with his or her phone. No more friends talking, no more families sitting together for fellowship. Dad, mother, children, everybody is connected to their phone. That phone occupies all our life 24-7. You can think about this. All the time you had with your family is gone, and the time you had to fellowship with your God is gone.

Your life is being controlled by a simple phone you bought with your own money.

Ask yourself, What is so important in your phone that makes you give way all the good time you had before that phone and find out those people who die in car accidents because they can't wait a second without their phone? It's true that the devil comes to steal. Do you know how much he has stolen from our families and our community?

The technology is very good and very important because sometimes it solves the problems very quickly. However, the devil hijacked it; the wicked evil activities are moving fast through technology. Today, you don't need to think through; you just ask Google which gives you the answer as quickly as you need it. But nice as it sounds, you cannot imagine how much evil goes through mass media and other technology.

In these days, we are in a season where we are moving and living in the midst of confusion made worse by false prophets and false teachers and the evil spirits rampant in very high places. We ask ourselves where the body of Christ stands in this situation. This is about you and me; do you know where you are? And do you know which side you are standing on today? Because of the strong winds and storms of new waves, Jesus is telling you to keep and protect what you have.

12

When Will the World Order Start Working?

World order is one of the signs of the end of the world as we are about to see in a few examples out of the many. Let us share about the world order.

Most people believe that the world order and the Antichrist will come lastly at the end of the world when everything is over. But in this book, you will find out that the world order has a lot of signs which are very clear for the coming of our Lord Jesus.

What we see today happening relates with combinations in the Word of God. You will believe how sooner rather than later the coming of Jesus will be because the world order is in place working already and is with us today as we mentioned that everything about the coming of our Lord Jesus is happening before our eyes.

This time, we are going to talk about numbers that are involved in world order, but this time, we won't go into details. World order system is already working worldwide. What identifies the world order is numbers, and these numbers unify the world. They are new laws which are governing the whole world. There are laws which govern the world today, and more laws are just waiting to be implemented. In this book, on this topic of world order, we are talking about the numbers only; next time, we will go into details. The 666

Antichrist numbers are in place today. Millions of chips of the number are already operational and are in use. More chips are in stores waiting for distribution, and some are already in our cities. How do these chips enter our countries and our communities?

Today, everyone and each person is identified by a number, and every business, organization, individual, each house has a number. Each country has a number called a code number to identify it, and zip code numbers identify the area and even your house number while every business in the world today must have an ID number. As you read this book, you must have personal ID, and your ID must have a number.

As you all know, there is nowhere you can pay taxes in the whole world without a TIN number or social security number. Nobody worldwide without these numbers above can deal with any bank or get a bank account. You must have those identification numbers before you do anything. As it was long prophesied, you will neither buy nor sell without a number.

Today, everybody from the newborn baby to the elderly you know must have an identification number. And the numbers will identify each person than a name of person.

> This also forced all people, great and small, rich and poor, free and slave, to receive a mark on their right hands or on their foreheads so that they could not buy or sell unless they had the mark, which is the name of the beast? Or the number of its name. (Revelation 13:16–17)

In today's life, nobody is forced to get the number. People are looking for the number for themselves because everybody is caught in that same trap of buying and selling. Everybody want to leave. With this trap, you can leave without job, without bank account— no life without number. It's because everything you need in life is already given with number. The numbers are already set. They just locate the number to you whenever you go for every service you need in your daily life.

What about your car number plate, it must be matched with your ID number and driver's license number and other numbers you have. Do you remember always and all the time you are asked about your date of birth? Those numbers that give out the day you were born mean a lot more than what you think. When you check properly, your date of birth and the month plus the year, they are six figures. They could be eight figures to cater for those with double figure birthdays and dates. They could be eight figures to cater for those with double figures, birthdays and dates. For example, a person born on the second of May 1964 equals 251964 which is equals to six digits. Every baby born today is born in the world of numbers. And each number he receives will stay on his name until the time of his death.

At this time, we won't talk much or go deep into figures and numbers. No man can fathom God's wisdom. What is important is that these numbers identify you—your name, your age, and everything about you everywhere and wherever you are in any country in the whole world. If you still think of the world order as something very far, you need to wake up. The world order is already with us today. When you look around, everything goes with numbers. Everywhere in the world today, people are very busy applying the numbers for their businesses and numbers for their taxes.

Since each one of us has these numbers, and we don't know where all these are heading to, it's important that we recognize the fact that they are already operating very fast, and we have gone farther than we think or know. There are a lot of evidence relating to the prophetic nature of numbers, and these are among the most significant signs of the end of the word. Suffice it to say, almost all human activities that revolve around economics and finance must have a number. We will get to know more about these numbers in the next part of our book.

13

Wars and Rumors of Wars before His Coming

When our Lord Jesus was explaining in His Word about the end of the world to His disciples, among the many signs He pointed out were wars and rumors of wars.

> And you will hear of wars and rumors of wars.
> See that you are not alarmed, for this must take
> place, but the end is not yet. (Matthew 24:6)

Have you heard or watched today's news? Every day, everywhere in all daily newspapers and TV stations, the news is about wars and rumors of war on a daily basis. The Bible talks about hearing rumors of wars, but if you can agree with me, today we are not only hearing rumors of war, but we are living in wars wherever we are in different parts of the globe. Can all this be a mere accident?

Today, it is not nation fighting against nation only; we have come to the level of tribe against tribe from the same country as family violence has reached scary heights. Even countries where there are no wars, people are killing each other day in and day out. To know the truth, find out what is happening in your country on your continent, and as you read, think about the Middle East which used to boast of a lot of peace and wealth, what is happening today in those

Arab countries, wars, death and destruction is the only news they have.

One time, Jesus was asked about this season of the end-times, and below are the words of the infallible Savior:

> Jesus answered: "Watch out that no one deceives you. For many will come in my name, claiming, 'I am the Messiah,' and will deceive many. You will hear of wars and rumors of wars, but see to it that you are not alarmed. Such things must happen, but the end is still to come. Nation will rise against nation and kingdom against kingdom. There will be famines and earthquakes in various places." (Matthew 24:4–7)

In verse 5, Jesus says, "Many will come in my name." This is happening today; in each and every country, you find many who are behaving the way Jesus said they would do—every evil and lie they do and tell it in His name. Many are doing miracles and healing people, but it is for their own glory.

Related to verse 6, we used to hear of wars and killings in Third World countries. Today, no country is left out. And most kingdoms within the same country fight each other as well.

> Brother will betray brother to death and a father his child. Children will rebel against their parents and have them put to death. (Mark 13:12)

Do you know that within families, they are fighting against families, fighting within the body of Christ as church, and fighting in companies? Remember, when a country has good family values and good church values, those make a nation of peace.

As Jesus illustrated regarding the end of the world, He said that we don't have to be alarmed that such things must happen. So when we see what is happening today, it gives us strong belief in His Word that all He said has to happen. Everything as it was prophesied about His coming is happening everywhere on every continent before our eyes. To some of us, our comfort zone is blinding us so we cannot see what season and time we are in today. It seems the church is slumbering behind the times.

The spirit of death is moving everywhere. Shootings and killings are widespread in many cities in different countries day by day.

When you hear about the suicide bomber, that means someone who has already decided to commit suicide willingly but does not believe in dying alone. But he is so demented he enjoys killing many other innocent people to die along with him.

As you read this book, please ask the Spirit of God to reveal more about His coming than what is written in this book.

Before you put this book down, please take a moment of prayer, and try to listen to what the Spirit of God is speaking to you about your personal relationship with Him. Please, listen to the soft voice of the Spirit, and hear what He is saying to your heart. My son/daughter don't give up I'm still in love with you be ready and clear your ways very soon I'm coming back for you.

14

The Church as Body of Christ Needs to Wake Up and Change

The church should redesign itself and come back to the truth of the Word of God. As things are changing very fast, the church should be faster to turn back to the foundation of Christ. The church is getting off from the foundation of Christ because of the new changes taking place in the world today. Because of that time when you fell off from the foundation, the Bible says:

> For other foundation can no man lay than that is laid, which is Jesus Christ. Now if any man builds upon this foundation gold, silver, precious stones, wood, hay, stubble; Every man's work shall be made manifest: for the day shall declare it, because it shall be revealed by fire; and the fire shall try every man's work of what sort it is. (1 Corinthians 3:11–13)

As we mentioned earlier about counterfeit gospel, today we have a lot of gospel full of diverse messages different from the real communication from our Lord Jesus Christ. These messages are being preached with emotions, loud, excitingly in seemingly charismatic speeches or calmly with a soft voice. It sound good to our ears, but let us see what the word of God say:

> For if someone comes to you and preaches a Jesus other than the Jesus we preached, or if you receive a different spirit from the Spirit you received, or a different gospel from the one you accepted, you put up with it easily enough. I do not think I am in the least inferior to those "super-apostles." (2 Corinthians 11:4–5)

Do you know how many preachers today preach another gospel which is not of our Lord Jesus in our congregations? Can you count how many are operating in the spirit which Apostle Paul talked about? Do you know how many preach a new doctrine? Do know it is this which hinders many people from hearing the gospel of Jesus Christ they earlier accepted?

In verse 5, Apostle Paul is again talking about the super apostles: those who thought they were more Christian than others (self-righteousness spirit). It is almost the same today when we have many who feel and believe they are super apostles, ministers, and all-powerful. They are highly respected and very proud of being popular.

My friend, you should come back from those other false messages which are being preached and come back to the true message of the cross.

The message of the cross is the reason Jesus came into our world—the message which changes a dying soul to a living soul, changes the darkness to light; the message changes the seed from inside man's heart to bear outside fruits. The message of the cross was not written to change people from one religion to another but to change men from death to life.

We are talking about the message which changed the fishermen and tax collectors to apostles. My fellow minister, when you preach on radio, TV, mass media, or in church, what kind of gospel are you preaching when you stand in front of God's people? It's high time we came back to what Jesus said to His disciples: "Go and teach what I taught you to all mankind." That was a very clear command to each and everybody who preaches the gospel of Jesus Christ.

> Teaching them to observe all things whatsoever
> I have commanded you: and, lo, I am with you
> always, even unto the end of the world [Amen].
> (Matthew 28:20)

All of us are under that same commissioning of our Lord Jesus Christ who knew that His disciples needed specific guidelines. Jesus knew about the many other teachings that would come up which would differ from His teaching.

And our Lord Jesus knew all this would happen in the days before His coming back. He said that when the time comes for His people to wait for Him, they will be slumbering and sleeping, and then the enemy will come in with other teachings the enemy comes in and plant another seed which is growing in church and confuse the people of God. As you read this book, think of how you should return to your foundation—to the true gospel of the cross that comes from Jesus Christ. The word of God says,

> The Lord was very angry with your ancestors. Therefore tell the people: This is what the Lord Almighty says: "Return to me," declares the Lord Almighty, "and I will return to you," says the Lord Almighty. Do not be like your ancestors to whom the earlier prophets proclaimed: This is what the Lord Almighty says: "Turn from your evil ways and your evil practices." But they would not listen or pay attention to me, declares

the Lord. Where are your ancestors now? And the prophets, do they live forever? But did not my words and my decrees, which I commanded my servants the prophets, overtake your ancestors? (Zechariah 1:2–6)

This scripture reminds us about our departed ancestors. They had an opportunity to obey God's word and do it, but they didn't, and consequently, they died. You and I still have this opportunity to believe; obey and live.

In all these scriptures and in every generation, God repeatedly asked His people to return back to Him. Now, it's our time. You and I should turn back to Him right now! This is our trumpet warning for us to change before He comes, and then tomorrow it will be too late.

Even the stork in the sky knows her appointed seasons, and the dove, the swift and the thrush observe the time of their migration. But my people do not know the requirements of the Lord. How can you say, "We are wise, for we have the law of the Lord," when actually the lying pen of the scribes has handled it falsely? (Jeremiah 8:7–8)

Sometimes when we go through hardship, some people think that God has forgotten about us. The truth you need to know is that our God is bigger than time. Yesterday, today, and forever is the same. He can't forget us; maybe we forget all about Him. He loves you and I, and He is coming soon. As the word of God says, "As God's coworkers, we urge you not to receive God's grace in vain."

This is what the Lord says: "In the time of my favor I will answer you, and in the day of salvation I will help you; I will keep you and will make you to be a covenant for the people, to restore the land and to reassign its desolate inheritances, to say to the captives, 'Come out,' and to those in darkness, 'Be free!' They will feed beside the roads and find pasture on every barren hill." (Isaiah 49:8–9)

When the Word of God says today, it's now; as you read this book, He is speaking to your heart again and again this is another God's favor to you as you read this book don't miss it.

As God's coworkers, we urge you not to receive God's grace in vain. For he says,

In the time of my favor I heard you, and in the day of salvation, I helped you. I tell you, now is the time of God's favor, and now is the day of salvation. (2 Corinthians 6:2)

15

What Do We Need to Do to Fight Back?

We have to stand firm in our faith. You have to know that when the Bible tells us about a good fight of faith, it means faith involves battle, and our faith is under attack. Therefore, we have to stand and fight and take hold of what we believe which we were called to do when we made our good confession in the presence of God and many witnesses.

> Fight the good fight of the faith. Take hold of the eternal life to which you were called when you made your good confession in the presence of many witnesses. In the sight of God, who gives life to everything, and of Christ Jesus, who while testifying before Pontius Pilate made the good confession, I charge you to keep this command without spot or blame until the appearing of our Lord Jesus Christ. (1 Timothy 6:12–14)

That is why we ask ourselves, what we are going to do after going through all these truths.

When you see the people in high authorities, the powerful countries passes the law which legalize the sin, that is what the Bible call the fight with high authorities in high places.

They use a law as weapon to fight; when the law passes, its done regardless of what the Word of God say about it. Whether it's evil, sin, or bad, it has become legal; the sin gets legal rights from the ruling spirits in high places. At that time, everybody ends up keeping quite or you face persecution, and sin get first seat and platform.

We are living in a spiritual war. It's a spiritual battle. Therefore, we have to do what we are supposed to do in this serious situation of fighting. What can we do before it gets too late?

That is why we ask ourselves, what are we going to do after going through all these truths about the soon coming of our Lord Jesus and the truth of our personal life and relationship with our God and our ministries?

We have to fight back; we are more than conquerors in Christ Jesus, and who is in us is more powerful than who is in the world. The word of God says of our warfare:

> For though we live in the world, we do not wage war as the world does. The weapons we fight with are not the weapons of the world. On the contrary, they have divine power to demolish strongholds. We demolish arguments and every pretension that sets itself up against the knowledge of God, and we take captive every thought to make it obedient to Christ. (1 Corinthians 10:3–5)

And everything attacks us; we have to fight and struggle against them all but not in the flesh, always when it is fighting means fighting and when it's a battle it is a battle, no compromising that's why the Bible talks about putting on full armor, mean to dressing up ready to fight spiritual Battle.

> For our struggle is not against flesh and blood, but against the rulers, against the authorities, against the powers of this dark world and against the spiritual forces of evil in the heavenly realms. Therefore put on the full armor of God, so that when the day of evil comes, you may be able to stand your ground, and after you have done everything, to stand. Stand firm then, with the belt of truth buckled around your waist, with the breastplate of righteousness in place. (Ephesians 6:12–14)

We are fighting in high places; the authorities in power give the evil a seat and permits it to be legalized.

When you hear His word, don't wait for more trumpets. It's today!

God again set a certain day, calling it *today*. This he did when a long time later, he spoke through David, as in the passage already quoted.

> Today, if you hear his voice, do not harden your hearts. (Hebrews 4:7)

As you read this book, take serious steps of changing and putting everything right. Do this in ministry, your church, in your personal life, and anything you do that is not based on the will of God who you serve before it's too late. Because He is coming, and His coming is very close, and it is becoming closer each day in our life.

This is your time to change as you are waiting for Him. This time of waiting for the coming of our Lord Jesus is the only opportune time to change, and at the same time, put more oil in our lamps (touch) for indeed the Bridegroom is coming soon…that is what we understand from the parable of the virgins.

At that time the kingdom of heaven will be like ten virgins who took their lamps and went out to meet the bridegroom. Five of them were foolish and five were wise. The foolish ones took their lamps but did not take any oil with them. The wise ones, however, took oil in jars along with their lamps. The bridegroom was a long time in coming, and they all became drowsy and fell asleep. At midnight the cry rang out: "here's the bridegroom! Come out to meet him!" Then all the virgins woke up and trimmed their lamps. The foolish ones said to the wise, "Give us some of your oil; our lamps are going out." "No," they replied, "there may not be enough for both us and you. Instead, go to those who sell oil and buy some for yourselves." (Matthew 25:1–9)

As you read this book, you need to understand that nobody and no one, not even husband or your daddy has somebody's oil; nobody has your oil. Each one of us has to be with his or her own. As the Bible says, each one of us has our reward from Jesus. And each one of us carries our own oil. Please hear, what is the Spirit talking to you?

In verse 5, when the bridegroom tarried, they all slumbered and slept. This scripture defines us and our time and the days of waiting we are going through today as a church. We are waiting. Some are almost giving up to sleep and fall off like Icarus who fell off the window during Peter's sermon.

This book is for the body of Christ, for all of us to read and hear the trumpet of His coming and wake up. It's not time to slumber and sleep; it's time to wake up, and change our ways to right ways. It's time to fill up our lamps with sufficient oil. If you do it now, it won't take long for you to be considered among the wise virgins.

In verse 9, the wise ones were telling the foolish that there may not be enough for both us and you. They advised them to instead go to those who sell oil and buy some for themselves. This is a wake-up call for everybody to know. What you need today is your own oil, not your friend's oil and not the relative's oil. It is your personal oil—your personal relation with God.

As Jesus said I'm coming back with reward for each one of you, the same way we need enough oil, each one of us. When He comes and finds you without enough oil, there will be no time to look or to buy oil for yourself. You have to use this remaining time, the only chance and opportunity, and as you are waiting for him, fill up your oil before He comes. You have to review what you have been doing and what you are doing now.

As we conclude our *Trumpet of His Coming*, these are the main points: Jesus is coming for the third time, and He is coming for you. Remember you need your oil for yourself. And the reward is for each one. This means that it is for you. It is not for a group or the name of a denomination.

That is why the scriptures say:

> Then two men will be in the field; one will be taken and one left. (Matt 24:40)

That means its individual; this taking of one man while leaving the other is a clear picture of how Jesus talks about a personality, not a group. Again, He still personalizes the enduring when He says:

> But the one who endures to the end will be saved. (Matthew 24:13)

The word said "the one" who endures, meaning it is a personal issue to endure. It is time to get out from the cover of a crowd and work out your endurance.

From this point on, we need to start with a serious determination and become a faithful servant, knowing that your master is standing beside you observing your work each day and each moment you can change your mindset and attitude about your ministry.

As you read this book, let your revival start within your heart, and it will flood like a river and flow over to all of your life, your ministry, and everything you are doing for the work of God.

Please don't take time to think about the author or writer of this book; rather, be focused on the message in the book which has the purpose of God to do good works in your life.

> As the word of God says: "For there is nothing hidden that will not be disclosed, and nothing concealed that will not be known or brought out into the open." (Luke 8:17)

Nothing was hidden in secret which will not be revealed. That is why we don't have to waste time in hiding and pretending because everything will come out publicly. As you read this book, please ask the Spirit of God to reveal to you more about His coming than is written in this book. In this book, there are some important scriptures I would like you to read and choose what you want to receive when He comes.

> Look, I am coming soon! My reward is with me, and I will give to each person according to what they have done. (Rev 22:12)

In this scripture, it personalizes the reward. When it mentions each person, it means each individual and person, not a group.

God is very serious about you! As He is coming, He must be with your reward, or He is going to say *I don't know you.* Today, you can choose what you want to receive or hear when He comes on that day.

For these words of Jesus, denying it is clear will be for prophets and those who cast out demons today.

> Many will say to me on that day, "Lord, Lord, did we not prophesy in your name and in your name drive out demons and in your name perform many miracles?" Then I will tell them plainly, "I never knew you. Away from me, you evildoers!"

Therefore, like the other virgins later also came.

> "Lord, Lord," they said, "open the door for us!" But he replied, "Truly I tell you, I don't know you."

Notice that the same way he personalized the reward is how he personalized the word, "I don't know you," not a group.

The same way is going to happen. Please don't wait to ask the door to be opened for you when it is too late, like the five virgins. The door is wide open for you today, right now!

Therefore keep watch, because you do not know the day or the hour.

Our Lord Jesus and the Holy Spirit love you and want so much to talk to you as His friend today. Before you put down this book, please take a moment of prayer, and try to listen to what the Spirit of God is speaking to you about your personal relationship with Him.

Please listen to what the Spirit is saying to your heart about your ministry.

It's high time for the church to turn back to the foundation of Jesus Christ and the foundation of the apostles and prophets after seeing all these signs of the coming back of our lord Jesus.

Please choose now to be waiting for the reward and not wait for rejection. You can have your own time to meditate upon the Word of God. He is willing to reveal to you more than what is written in this book. His desire to come back for you and find you well prepared like faithful servant waiting for his king or Bride waiting for Bridegroom.

If this book has helped you, please pass it to someone or recommend it to your friend, because everybody and each of us needs help. Be blessed.

About the Author

Bishop Joseph Karasanyi. along with his wife Rose Karasanyi. are founders and church planters of deliverance Churches in Rwanda Congo and other countries.

He received Christ in 1980 when Jesus appeared to him in his bedroom. And he started serving the Lord in 1982.

Bishop Joseph Karasanyi is the president and founder of *Restore Ministries* operating in many parts of Africa including Rwanda, Congo, Uganda, South Sudan, Ethiopia, and also in the Middle East.

With apostolic anointing, he has planted hundreds of churches in these countries. And he has also been busy promoting education through building Christian schools in different places.

Joseph is also the founder and CEO of JRK Ministries International based in Tulsa, Oklahoma, USA.

He has traveled extensively throughout Africa, Asia, the Middle East, Europe, the Caribbean islands, the USA, and more than fifty countries worldwide preaching the gospel of the Lord Jesus Christ.

He has organized large evangelical crusades all over Africa and the Middle East working with other evangelical ministries and international organizations.

Today, he has a message of Jesus's coming back and a ministry of awakening of ministers of the gospel to return to their roots and empowering the wounded ministers and frustrated gospel ministers not to give up their ministries, for their Master is at the door coming back soon!